W9-BGW-468

Ethics of Food

Catching and Raising Seafood

John Bliss

Heinemann Library
Chicago, Illinois

www.heinemannraintree.com
Visit our website to find out
more information about
Heinemann-Raintree books.

To order:
☎ Phone 888-454-2279
💻 Visit www.heinemannraintree.com
to browse our catalog and order online.

Edited by Adam Miller, Andrew Farrow, and Adrian
Vigliano
Designed by Ryan Frieson
Illustrated by Mapping Specialists, Ltd. and
Planman Technologies
Picture research by Tracy Cummins
Originated by Capstone Global Library Ltd.
Printed and bound in the United States of America
by Corporate Graphics in North Mankato,
Minnesota
15 14 13 12 11
10 9 8 7 6 5 4 3 2 1

**Library of Congress Cataloging-in-Publication
Data**
Cataloging-in-Publication data is on file at the
Library of Congress.

ISBN 978-1-4329-5102-3 (HB)
ISBN 978-1-4329-6192-3 (PB)

Acknowledgements

The author and publisher are grateful to the
following for permission to reproduce copyright
material: AP Photo pp. 11 (Brooke McDonald/Sea
Shepherd Conservation Society), 49 (Fiona Hanson/
PA Wire); Corbis p. 14 (© Natalie Fobes/Science
Faction); Getty Images pp. 19 (SAM YEH/AFP), 20
(Kim Steele), 31 (BEN BORG CARDONA/AFP),
36 (MIKE CLARKE/AFP), 39 (Win McNamee;
istockphoto p. 25 (© alvarez); National Geographic
Stock p. 28 (BILL CURTSINGER); Shutterstock pp.
10 (© DK.samco), 17 (© Chaikovskiy Igor), 22 (©
Konstantin Karchevskiy), 26 (© kevinhung), 33 (©
Mircea Bezergheanu), 40 (© Elzbieta Sekowska), 42
(© TororoReaction), 45 (© Elena Yakusheva), 47 (©
Olga Lyubkina); The Granger Collection, NYC p. 5.

Cover photograph of Atlantic Bluefin tuna being
loaded onto a Japanese processing ship, near
Barbate, Spain in 2002 reproduced with permission
of Corbis (© William Boyce).

We would like to thank Christopher Nicolson for
his invaluable help in the preparation of this book.

Every effort has been made to contact copyright
holders of any material reproduced in this book.
Any omissions will be rectified in subsequent
printings if notice is given to the publisher.

All the Internet addresses (URLs) given in this book
were valid at the time of going to press. However,
due to the dynamic nature of the Internet, some
addresses may have changed, or sites may have
changed or ceased to exist since publication. While
the author and publisher regret any inconvenience
this may cause readers, no responsibility for any
such changes can be accepted by either the author
or the publisher.

Contents

Some words are printed in bold, **like this**. You can find out what they mean by looking in the glossary.

Down to the Sea in Ships

On September 20, 1991, the fishing vessel *Andrea Gail* set sail from Gloucester, Massachusetts. It was headed for the Grand Banks, which are popular fishing grounds off the coast of Newfoundland, in Canada. The six-person crew was fishing for swordfish. Despite a threat of bad weather, the crew set out to sea, driven by the need to make a living.

After several weeks of poor fishing, the crew set sail for home. It is believed that they set out when they did in part because the boat's onboard ice machine had failed, threatening the freshness of the fish that had been caught—and the money they could make by bringing home a fresh catch.

On the way back to Gloucester, the *Andrea Gail* ran into what later became called the "perfect storm." This was a combination of a fast-moving storm called a cyclone off the northeast coast of the United States and the weakening storm of Hurricane Grace. Wind speeds reached 65 knots (about 121 kilometers per hour, or 75 miles per hour), with waves rising up to nearly 12 meters (40 feet). The *Andrea Gail* and its entire crew were lost at sea. (The story of the *Andrea Gail* became the basis of the book *The Perfect Storm*, which was made into a movie starring George Clooney and Mark Wahlberg.)

> "She's comin' on, boys, and she's comin' on strong."—The final transmission of Billy Tyne, captain of the *Andrea Gail*

The story of the *Andrea Gail* highlights many of the challenges faced by fishers today. Finding fish can be difficult under the best of conditions, and month-long voyages, like that of the *Andrea Gail*, are not uncommon. When facing competition from large **commercial** fishing **fleets**, smaller vessels like the *Andrea Gail* are also sometimes forced to put themselves in greater danger than they should. Fishing is a difficult and dangerous way to earn a living.

Fish tales

Fishing has been a subject of literature for hundreds of years. Readers are drawn to the stories of humans against nature, and the romance of the open sea has always been a draw. Some of the best-known novels are Herman Melville's *Moby-Dick* (1851), Rudyard Kipling's *Captains Courageous* (1897), and Ernest Hemingway's *The Old Man and the Sea* (1952).

For hundreds or years, fishing has been a dangerous way to make a living.

The fishing industry

In the past, after fishers caught seafood, they primarily sold it locally. People ate fish or shellfish from nearby oceans, lakes, and streams. Those who lived far from bodies of water simply did not eat much seafood. Today, however, modern freezing and shipping technology allows people to enjoy seafood around the world.

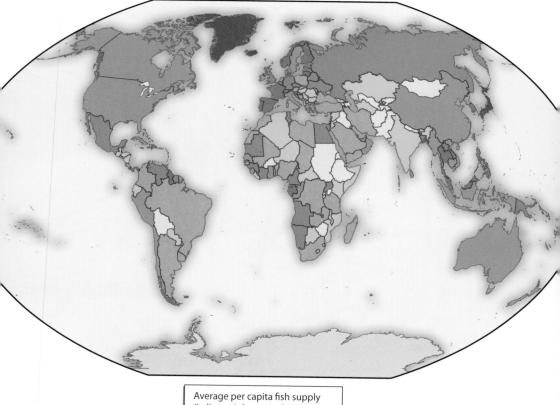

Average per capita fish supply
(in liveweight equivalent)

☐	0–2 kg/year	◼	20–30
◼	2–5	◼	30–60
◼	5–10	◼	60+
◼	10–20	☐	No data

Fish caught and farmed in Asia, North America, South America, and Europe find their way to dinner plates around the world.

The modern fishing industry is a big business. According to the Food and Agriculture Organization of the United Nations (FAO), in 2005 the harvest by commercial **fisheries** around the world was nearly 90.7 million tonnes (100 million tons). China was the biggest producer, accounting for a third of the world's production. About 90 percent of that figure represents saltwater fish, with the rest caught inland. Due to modern transportation methods, most fish are now consumed far from where they were caught. Fish caught in the Mediterranean Sea may end up on the table in a sushi restaurant in Japan.

In addition to fish caught in the wild, **aquaculture**, or the farming of fish, is a growing business (see pages 18 to 19). In 2005 fish farms accounted for another 45.3 million tonnes (50 million tons) of seafood. As the number of fish in the wild fall due to **overfishing** (fishing too much of one kind of fish; see pages 24 to 29) and **pollution** (see pages 34 to 39), aquaculture has become more and more vital.

Making choices

As we will see throughout this book, while **consumers** have greater options than ever before, they also face many **ethical** choices. They need to be aware of **species** that are facing extinction (dying out) due to overfishing. And with the growing dangers of **toxins** (poisons) in the water, people should educate themselves about which fish are safe to eat. Finally, consumers have to realize and accept the role they play in the fishing industry.

Environment watch

Overfishing—an old problem

Overfishing is not a recent problem in human history, although the problem has become more severe as more and more people have populated all corners of the globe. Human history is also a history of overfishing. By the late−1400s in Europe, people had already overfished most of the inland lakes and rivers, as well as coastal areas. One of the more amazing and valuable things explorers and colonizers of the New World found was an abundance of seafood, both inland and in the sea off the coasts. It didn't take long before the inland and coastal waters of the Americas also suffered from overfishing.

Eating Seafood

Seafood is one of the healthiest parts of many people's diets. This has been the case throughout history.

Dining trends

Records show that ancient Egyptians, Greeks, and Romans all fished their local waters. But the popularity of seafood has grown and changed throughout the years.

In the past, **mollusks** such as clams and oysters were eaten by working-class people who dug them from the sand or harvested them from the ocean. Lobster, too, was a food of the common person. Lobster was eaten at the first thanksgiving in North America—not because it was a treat, but rather because it was so plentiful. Today, shellfish such as these sell for a high price and are consumed as luxury items.

> "He was a bold man that first ate an oyster."
> —Jonathan Swift, Irish author

Prehistoric fishing

Even our earliest of ancestors fished. There's evidence that **Neanderthals** traveled to the coast of Spain as much as 30,000 years ago to hunt and fish for seafood such as mussels, mollusks, fish, seals, and dolphins. **Paleontologists** have found evidence suggesting that Neanderthals made visits to the coast of Spain specifically during breeding seasons when sea mammals came to shore, catching large numbers of young seals and dolphins. Damaged bones and evidence of a hearth for a fire show that they were able to heat the meat and separate it from the bones.

Seafood today

Humans need water and have often settled near it. Seas and rivers were the earliest highways. Fresh water is essential for drinking. And seafood was plentiful in the world's waters, until populations increased and overfishing became an ever more serious issue. Today seafood is as popular as ever worldwide. Worldwide consumption of seafood has grown steadily since the end of World War Two (1939–1945). The production of seafood grew from 19 million tonnes (21 million tons) in 1950 to 130 million tonnes (143 million tons) in 2001. The use of refrigeration in modern times while transporting fresh fish has even allowed people worldwide to enjoy the Japanese traditions of sushi and sashimi, which are methods of serving raw, fresh fish.

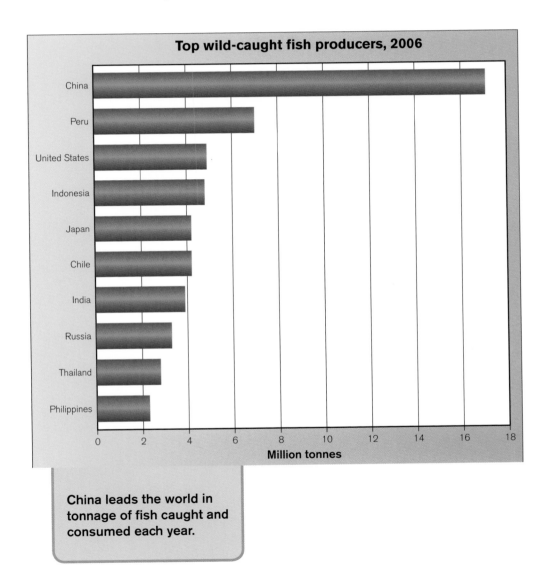

Top wild-caught fish producers, 2006

Million tonnes

China leads the world in tonnage of fish caught and consumed each year.

Sushi and raw foods

Sushi most likely came to Japan from China in the 7th century. Sushi includes sticky rice and raw fish, and sashimi is simply raw fish. Over the past 20 years, sushi bars have sprung up all around the world. Sushi, or raw fish, has become so popular that many people no longer think of it as an ethnic food, but rather as a **staple** food, alongside pizza and tacos. In fact, many chefs now make the rolls with ingredients far removed from those that are traditional in Japan, such as avocado and mozzarella cheese.

In the past 20 years, new sushi restaurants have sprung up all around the world.

Health watch

The health risks of sushi

There can be a risk to eating sushi. A California roll, which contains crab and avocado, can hold 400 calories and 2 grams of salt. Raw tuna can hold **parasites** like worms, which can cause stomach pain and other problems. Even if the fish has been frozen, as required by many countries, people who are sensitive to worms can still have reactions.

Sushi also has hidden costs to the environment and workers. Tuna caught in the Mediterranean Sea is **processed** in large factory-like plants that dot the sea. These kinds of factories pollute the oceans. Trucks haul in loads of fish from surrounding fisheries. Overworked employees covered in fish blood slaughter, gut, and pack the fish in factory-like conditions. The processed fish are shipped to airports, where they are flown to restaurants and markets around the world. What was once a healthy treat is becoming a new "fast food."

Perhaps fueled by recent interest in sushi, the latest dining trend is toward all kinds of raw fish. Crudo is one such raw preparation. "Crudo" means "raw" in Italian. Crudo has been popular in Italy for generations, but it has just caught on in other countries. Traditional crudo is raw fish drizzled with olive oil and paired with other flavors, such as salt and lemon. Modern restaurants now offer crudo with everything from almond oil to pickled radish.

Other raw fish dishes include tartare, in which the fish is chopped, and ceviche, in which the fish is "cooked" in the acid from citrus fruits, such as lemons and limes. As with any raw preparation, it is important that only the freshest fish is used. Otherwise, diners could become ill.

What do you think?

Dolphin hunting

In some parts of the world, people eat whale and dolphin meat. Although the practice is largely barred in the West, some Asian fishers still hunt these sea mammals, a tradition that dates back at least 400 years. Western nations have sought to end this trade.

"People say dolphins are cute and smart, but some regions have a tradition of eating dolphin meat," said Toshinori Uoya, a Japanese fisheries official. "Dolphin-killing may be bad for our international image, but we can't just issue an order for it to stop."

Is killing dolphins for meat a cruel practice that should stop? Or should it be accepted as a cultural difference? Is there a middle ground that can satisfy both sides?

In recent years, the Japanese practice of hunting dolphins has received attention in the West.

The health benefits of seafood

Scientific research over the past 30 years has uncovered many of the health benefits of a diet high in seafood. **Protein** is an essential nutrient for human health, and it is found throughout your body. Seafood is a good, healthy source of protein in your diet—recommended to be included twice a week. However, in most western countries, including the United States, seafood still ranks far below other meats in terms of protein consumption.

For years, doctors have known about the link between fish consumption and lower rates of heart disease. In recent years, research has focused on **omega-3 fatty acids**. Like other animals, fish store energy in the form of fat. While mammals such as cows store energy in saturated fats, which have been linked to heart disease, fish fats and oils are mostly unsaturated fats. Omega-3 fatty acids—named for their chemical composition—are thought to lower the amounts of cholesterol and triglycerides in the blood. These are two substances that increase the risk

What does frozen versus fresh fish mean to me?

Unless you live on the coast, you probably have access to a greater variety of frozen fish than fresh fish. That is not a bad thing. Fish caught for immediate sale at fish markets are generally stored on ice in large bins on fishing vessels. Larger ships **flash freeze** their catch for shipping to stores. Flash freezing is a process in which food is quickly frozen using super-cooled air. Because the freezing process happens so quickly—much more quickly than food stored in a home freezer—large ice crystals do not have a chance to form. Since it is these large crystals that damage flesh, the fish are almost perfectly preserved. For this reason, flash-frozen fish may be "fresher" than fresh fish stored on ice.

Health watch

The Mediterranean diet

People are always looking for healthier ways to eat and new plans for losing weight. In the 1970s, the "Mediterranean diet" became popular. Many news stories focused on the healthy effects of olive oil, garlic, and red wine. They often overlooked other elements of the diet of Mediterranean countries, which include smaller portions, lots of fresh fruits and vegetables—and plenty of fish.

of heart disease. Omega-3 fats are also rich in antioxidants. Antioxidants are chemicals that help clean the blood of dangerous substances.

Fish oils have also been shown to increase brain function and improve the health of joints. Recent research shows that older people who eat more oily fish are able to think faster and remember more than those who do not. These same fish oils seem to help young people with attention-deficit hyperactivity disorder (ADHD) improve their concentration and reading skills. Recent studies have even linked consumption of fish oils to lower rates of cancer.

Unfortunately, eating fish can also include some risks. In recent years, some fish—particularly larger fish, such as tuna—have shown high levels of **mercury** and other chemicals (see pages 34 and 35).

Health watch

Mercury levels in fish

Nearly all fish contain traces of mercury, but fish that contain high levels of mercury can harm your health and should be avoided whenever possible. Use this chart as a basic guide to help avoid fish that are high in mercury:

Mercury content by fish type		
Low mercury (eat regularly)	Moderate mercury (eat moderately)	High mercury (avoid eating)
Anchovies	Cod	Grouper
Catfish	Halibut	Marlin
Herring	Mahi-mahi	Orange roughy
Salmon	Skate	Swordfish
Sardines	Tuna	Shark

Industrial Fishing

Many countries have large fishing industries. Among the world leaders are the United States, Japan, China, Russia, Peru, and India. The top-producing countries account for more than half of the world's production. China alone accounts for one-third of the world's production.

While small fishing fleets still operate, most fishing today is a big business. In 2008 fisheries in the United States contributed approximately $35 billion a year to the economy. Global fisheries generated more than $84.9 billion in 2004.

Trawling

Trawling is the method of capture used by most fisheries. Trawling is dragging a net through the ocean. The two most popular methods are bottom trawling, which is drawing a net along the sea bottom, and midwater trawling, in which the net is drawn higher up in the sea. Anything in the field of the net gets drawn in, and it is all later sorted onboard the ship.

Sonar

Modern technology has helped fishing vessels target large schools of fish more efficiently. **Sonar** devices use sound waves underwater to locate objects.

Trawlers like this use large nets to haul in their catch.

Some fishing ships use fish attracting devices, or FADs, to draw fish to the ship. FADs are large floating objects lowered into the water. This method works because many species of fish tend to gather near large objects, such as buoys or shipwrecks. Other fish tend to gather near larger sea creatures. For example, tuna often gather near dolphins. This is one reason why tuna fishing is often so dangerous to dolphin populations.

Other techniques

In some countries, fishers even use dynamite or poisons such as cyanide to catch fish. Cyanide stuns the fish, rather than killing them, and many fish caught this way are sold to aquariums. The cyanide is deadly to other creatures, though, including the coral that create coral reefs. Blast fishing—fishing with explosives—is also destructive to these environments. In the Philippines, for example, blast fishing has destroyed many coral reefs.

Environment watch

Bottom trawling and the destruction of habitats

Bottom trawling has been particularly destructive to fish **habitats**, or natural environments. Over the past 100 years, populations of bottom-living fish have dropped terribly, and the seabed **ecosystems** of the North Atlantic have completely changed. There is no way to predict the future health of these environments.

What do you think?

Controlling the practices of other nations

Most nations have banned destructive fishing practices. How can those nations get nations such as the Philippines, which still use such practices, to stop? Do powerful countries, such as the United States and the United Kingdom, have the right to interfere with another nation's fishing practices?

Factory ships

The largest commercial fishing vessels are like floating factories. They not only catch fish, but they also process and freeze the catch. They have state-of-the-art technology, such as sonar, that can pinpoint schools of fish quickly and accurately. Like factories on land, many of the functions of a factory ship are automated, allowing them to operate more efficiently. The FAO estimates that there are more than 38,000 fishing vessels that weigh more than 90 tonnes (100 tons) working the seas.

Unlike smaller vessels, factory ships carry large crews and stay at sea for weeks at a time. Some even serve as mother ships for fleets of smaller vessels. These smaller ships trawl the ocean for their catch and then return to the mother ship, where the fish are processed.

Factory ships are equipped to process fish completely. The catch is sorted, and the **bycatch**—whatever else comes up in the nets—is returned to the ocean. The fish are then transferred to the processing deck. Here, they are gutted and have their heads removed. The flesh is flash frozen, often in individual portions. Parts of the fish that cannot be sold for human consumption, such as the heads, bones, and guts, are processed into fish meal. Fish meal is dried and ground fish that is used as feed for animals and as **fertilizer** to help crops and plants grow.

What do you think?

The dangers of commercial fishing

Commercial fishing is dangerous work. In the United States, fishers are more likely to die at work than members of any other profession. In 2008 the U.S. workforce overall averaged 3.6 work-related deaths per 100,000 employees. In commercial fishing, though, there were nearly 130 deaths per 100,000 workers. More than half of those deaths were a result of boats sinking, and nearly 30 percent were a result of crew members being washed overboard. Eight percent were from accidents on deck. It is not getting any safer. Because of the recent slow-down in the economy, work-related deaths dropped for most occupations in 2008—but not for fishing. In 2007, 38 fishers died, and 50 died in 2008.

Since commercial fishing is such a dangerous job, should it even continue? How can it be made safer? Should government play a greater role in **regulating** commercial fishing?

Large fishing vessels often drag up more than just fish. Unfortunately, much of the bycatch—which includes other fish, turtles, sharks, and sea mammals such as dolphins—often die in the nets or on the deck of the ship. In addition, because these vessels are so large and so efficient, they have played a major role in overfishing the oceans. For these reasons, some people oppose their use.

Giant factory ships like this one work to process enormous amounts of seafood. One of the largest ships currently in use is the *Atlantic Dawn*. This ship is able to process a whopping 350 tonnes (385 tons) of fish a day, carry 3,300 tonnes (3,000 tons) of fuel, and store 7,700 tonnes (7,000 tons) of graded and frozen catch.

Seafood from a Farm

You have read about industrial fisheries that harvest seafood from the sea. But a growing amount of seafood consumed around the world is not caught from fisheries such as these, but is actually farmed. "Aquaculture" is the term that describes raising fish and other kinds of seafood for food in an environment operated or controlled by humans. Along with finfish, such as salmon and tilapia, many mollusks and crustaceans, such as clams, oysters, scallops, and shrimp, are now raised in large numbers on aquaculture farms.

The benefits of farmed seafood

Aquaculture is the fastest-growing food production system in the world. The industry has grown at a strong and steady 8 to 10 percent over the past three decades and many people expect that this trend of expansion will continue at that rate for a while. Aquaculture-raised fish and seafood also help to provide a significant source of protein for people in many countries around the world. Globally, as much as half of the seafood consumed by humans is now produced by seafood farms instead of being caught in traditional fisheries.

There are many benefits to the aquaculture approach of raising seafood. In recent years, the increasing worldwide demand for seafood has led to an increase in overfishing, which has **depleted** (emptied) or drastically reduced the amount of wild seafood in many natural fisheries. Raising fish and other kinds of seafood in aquaculture environments provides an alternative source of seafood to help satisfy global demand. In addition, seafood farming provides jobs for people around the world, particularly in Asian countries.

Some seafood, such as carp, are able to adapt surprisingly well to farming environments. In fact, more carp are raised through aquaculture than any other fish. Smaller freshwater fish, such as catfish and trout, live in crowded environments in the wild. These fish have also adapted very well to aquaculture farming ponds. As long as these animals are fed and raised responsibly, the farmed versions of these fish are very similar to those caught in the wild.

Health watch

Cobia: The new cod?

Cod has long been a staple of commercial fishing. But with cod **stocks** (numbers) severely depleted, marketers are always on the lookout for a fish that could serve as its replacement. Cobia (pictured here) may fit the bill.

Like cod, cobia has firm, white flesh and high oil content. It is attractive to commercial fisheries because it grows very quickly. Cobia can grow 5 to 6 kilograms (11 to 13 pounds) in a year, while salmon takes 30 to 36 months to reach the same size. In the wild, cobia can grow up to 60 kilograms (132 pounds)—but most commercial cobia is farmed. Cobia farms are already active in Asia, and the Norwegian company Marine Farms is now farming the fish to sell at markets in Europe and the United States.

The dangers of farmed fish

While farmed fish present an alternative to fish harvested from the ocean, aquaculture presents problems of its own. One concern is the amount of food it takes to grow farmed fish. Popular large species, such as salmon and tuna, are **carnivorous**. In the wild, they live on other fish. In a farmed environment, they are fed fish meal, which is created from smaller fish. As we have seen, fish meal is made by drying and grinding the unusable parts of fish (see page 16).

What do you think?
Does cost matter?

Farm-raised fish are usually significantly cheaper than fish caught in the wild. Wild salmon can cost twice as much as farm-raised salmon. Despite the concerns about aquaculture, farm-raised fish such as salmon are still a good source of omega-3 fats and other important nutrients. How do you decide whether to buy wild or farm-raised fish? How should you weigh the benefits and drawbacks of each?

Some aquaculture operations have developed good health and environmental records.

Health and environment concerns

Seafood is a good source of protein. Wild seafood is good for you, but can be bad for the environment, depending on the place, type of seafood, and method of fishing.

Fish farming raises new concerns. What are the fish fed? How are they treated? Is the nutritional value of the seafood changed by farming? Are there consequences to the local environment? Many seafood farmers use **antibiotics** and pesticides to keep control over the health of their fish. But many studies show that these chemicals are not good for human health. In *Food Rules: An Eater's Manual*, Michael Pollan offers the following advice: "Fortunately, a few of the most nutritious wild fish species, including mackerel, sardines, and anchovies, are well managed, and in some cases are even abundant."

The problem is that it takes a lot of fish to make fish meal. To create 1 kilogram (2.2 pounds) of fish meal, it takes 4.5 kilograms (10 pounds) of smaller fish. In recent years, fish meal as feed for farmed fish has been replaced to some degree by grain. But while the percentage of fish used as feed has gone down, the number of fish produced has gone up, so there is still high demand for fish meal.

A related issue is the amount of food it takes to raise large carnivorous fish. Farm-raised tuna are fed live fish, such as anchovies and sardines. It takes about 20 kilograms (44 pounds) of fish to grow 1 kilogram (2.2 pounds) of tuna. Some people see this as a tremendous waste. Fish lower on the **food chain**, such as catfish and carp, are omnivorous, meaning they eat both meat and plants. It takes far fewer resources to feed these fish. Some people argue that these fish should be the focus of the fish farming industry.

Many fish in the oceans eat the same small fish that are fed to tuna and other large carnivores. There is a concern that overfishing these small fish may lead to a drop in the populations of other fish. In addition, many people eat sardines and anchovies as well. Using them to feed tuna is taking food out of our own mouths!

"A land with lots of herring can get along with few doctors."
—Dutch proverb

Aquaculture and the environment

Aquaculture can also have negative effects on the environment. Much farmed fish, especially large varieties such as salmon and tuna, are raised in cages or pens that are open to the sea. As a result, chemicals, waste, and disease can easily travel from the cages to the surrounding environment.

Because farmed fish live so close together, disease is common. Small parasites called sea lice (which are not related to the insects we know as lice) often infect salmon and trout.

Aquaculture pens that are open to the ocean can sometimes pollute surrounding waters.

Health watch

Are farmed fish healthy?

While they appear alike on the surface, wild and farmed fish can be very different. Because they live their lives in pens, farmed salmon have more fat than the wild varieties. But because they contain other, less beneficial fats, they may actually contain less of the omega-3 fats that make fish so healthy. In addition, since wild salmon eat a more varied diet than those raised on farms, they provide a wider range of nutrients.

Farmed fish may also contain high levels of antibiotics and pesticides, chemicals used to control the disease and parasites that can be a problem in fish farming. Some farmed salmon also contain high levels of chemicals called polychlorinated biphenyls (PCBs), which have been linked to cancer. PCBs are chemicals that are often found in fish food, and which are stored in fat cells. Since farm-raised fish have more fat than the wild varieties, they tend to contain more PCBs. For these reasons, health organizations recommend people limit farm-raised salmon to one serving per week.

Fish are treated either with a chemical bath or with special feed containing antibiotics intended to prevent illness. In either case, these chemicals can escape from open pens into the surrounding seawater. In addition, since fish farms are adjacent to wild fish habitats, diseases can spread easily from farmed to wild fish.

Other chemicals are used to clean and maintain enclosures. For example, special paints are used on pens. These contain toxic (poisonous) chemicals designed to keep plants, such as algae, from growing on the enclosures. Over time, these chemicals dissolve and are released into the surrounding waters, where they continue to kill off sea life.

Waste from farmed fish drops through the caged area to the sea floor below. Many fish farms are located in protected areas, such as coves, where water moves very slowly. As a result, the waste does not get washed away, as it would in the open ocean. This can lead to the buildup of bacteria on the sea floor. These bacteria kill off other microscopic plants and animals that normally live in the area, and which serve as food for larger creatures. As a result, this collection of waste can have long-ranging effects.

Where Have All the Fish Gone?

Oceans cover more than three-quarters of planet Earth. These bodies of water are home to more than 80 percent of all life on the planet. Millions of people depend on the oceans for food and income. Unfortunately, today this valuable resource is endangered because of ignorance and a global lack of management.

In simplest terms, overfishing is just that—catching so many fish that fish populations do not have a chance to replenish themselves. It is fishing in a way that is not **sustainable**, meaning it cannot be continued over time. The problem of overfishing affects all the people who depend on the sea for their livelihoods.

Case study:
The decline of the UK fishing industry

According to a study by the University of York and the Marine **Conservation** Society, both in the United Kingdom, UK trawlers caught twice as much fish in 1889 as they do today. In England and Wales, 19th-century fishing ships caught as much as four times as many fish as modern vessels. The UK fishing industry reached its peak in the 1930s. Since that time, the number of fish available for catch has fallen by 94 percent.

New fishing vessels travel much farther out to sea than 19th-century ships could. These new fishing areas, and the development of new fishing technology, have masked the decline of fish in UK waters. While fish stocks continue to fall, these methods allow the number of fish caught to remain fairly constant. Unfortunately, this simply serves to reduce those fish stocks that were previously untapped.

Case study:
Cod: The king of the sea

One shocking example of overfishing was the collapse of cod fisheries off the coast of Newfoundland in Canada.

Cod has been called "the fish that fed the world." For thousands of years, this white-fleshed fish was a staple of the diet of many civilizations. Atlantic cod fueled the voyages of the Vikings in the 8th to 10th centuries, allowing them to cross the ocean to North America. Since cod was easy to preserve through salting and drying, it served as a trade good throughout Europe. Norwegians introduced dried cod to southern Europe, where it quickly became a staple. Cod fishing played an important role in the development of the east coast of North America in the 17th and 18th centuries, and fishing grounds were widely disputed between the British and the French. Early colonists to the "New World" of North America settled in an area that was named Cape Cod because the fish were so plentiful. Cod continued to be central to the fishing trade into the 20th century.

But in 1992, the cod industry collapsed when it became apparent that there were simply no fish left. About 40,000 people lost their jobs. Canada banned cod fishing. In 2003 cod was placed on the **endangered species** list. Once a staple around the world, the future of cod remains uncertain.

Fish markets are one of the best sources for fresh fish. This worker is preparing a freshly caught tuna at a fish market in Tokyo, Japan.

What causes overfishing?

There are several factors that contribute to overfishing. One is the sheer size of the fleet of ships working the oceans. According to some experts, the global fishing fleet is 2.5 to 4 times as large as the oceans can manage. (The "global fishing fleet" includes all the ships that are fishing the seas.) Some fleets use more responsible methods than others. But overall, when facing the odds, the fish simply do not have a chance.

The damage caused by overfishing

As we have seen, trawling destroys many of the fish habitats on the ocean floor (see pages 14 and 15). These methods not only catch too many fish. They also ruin the environments where fish breed. In addition, as fish populations drop, younger and younger fish get caught up in commercial nets. As a result, fish are being pulled from the sea before they are old enough to breed. It is an ongoing cycle of destruction.

As natural predators in ocean food chains are overfished, populations of prey animals such as jellyfish can grow to unnaturally high levels.

The numbers are frightening. According to the UN, 52 percent of the world's fisheries are fished out. Another 24 percent are either in danger or recovering from collapse. Most of this destruction has occurred over the past 50 years.

As we continue to overfish our oceans, we change entire sea populations. About 90 percent of large predators, such as tuna, swordfish, and cod, have been fished out. By removing these predators, the number of their prey, such as jellyfish, grow to large proportions. They then deplete the populations of the smaller creatures they depend upon to survive. As a result, the entire ecosystem changes.

Case study:
The case of the Chilean sea bass

The Chilean sea bass is a marketing success story gone bad. It is neither a bass, nor is it primarily found in Chile. Until the late 1970s, it was called the Patagonian toothfish, a name that accurately describes this ugly species. The Chileans were the first to market toothfish commercially, which is how it got part of its new name. Chilean sea bass has firm, white meat that lends itself easily to a variety of preparations. Because of this, it became a very popular item in specialty markets and high-end restaurants.

As is often the case, the success of the Chilean sea bass was also its undoing. The fish lives for a long time—up to 50 years—and can grow up to 45 kilograms (100 pounds). But because it lives so long, it does not reach full maturity until it is 12 or 13 years old. In addition, it does not migrate (travel) to new areas. Most Chilean sea bass are born, live, and die in the same habitat. That makes it easy for fishers with long lines to catch lots of the fish. And since they mature slowly, many are caught before they are old enough to reproduce.

Desire for the fish was so strong that stocks were quickly overfished. Though the fish is not yet endangered, fishing it is heavily regulated. A commission of 24 countries has set catch limits and other controls. Still, some people estimate that twice as much of the fish is caught illegally as is caught legally (see pages 32 and 33). For these reasons, it is important that consumers and restaurant owners are aware of the source of the fish before they buy it.

Case study:
Peekytoe crab

Peekytoe crab is a hot item in many seafood restaurants. It sells for up to $20 a pound on the retail market. But until recently, it was only seen as a disposable bycatch.

Until 1997 peekytoes were called rock crabs, and they were caught in lobster traps off the coast of Maine. Because the crabs are small and hard to ship, they were either released or eaten in the homes of lobster fishers. Then Rod Mitchell, a seafood wholesaler, started marketing them as peekytoe crabs, its local slang name. Suddenly, they exploded in popularity.

Chefs love the crab for its delicate flavor, which they call sweet and fresh. Customers have learned to look for it by name. The story of the peekytoe crab is not only a brilliant marketing ploy, but also an example of how a once-useless bycatch can turn into a useful—and sustainable—product.

The peekytoe crab is an example of bycatch that became a useful product.

Bycatch

Bycatch is another issue related to overfishing. As previously discussed, bycatch refers to the fish and other sea creatures, such as dolphins and sea turtles, that are caught accidentally while harvesting another species. Bycatch is often returned to the sea, but by that time, the creatures may already be dead. According to a report by the international marine group Oceana, "Up to 3,000 tonnes (3,300 tons) of fish caught accidentally by fishing vessels in European waters is thrown back dead. Discards can reach 90 percent of the total weight of the catch in some fisheries."

This is seen as a waste of edible fish. The head of the European Commission Fisheries, Maria Damanaki, has said, "This is something we could afford when we had healthy stock, but now, when stocks are declining, nobody can justify that we take fish and because of our policy we force people to throw it back." Damanaki has suggested reducing the amount of time fishing fleets are allowed to fish for and closing mixed fisheries when the maximum quota of one species has been caught. Chef and food writer Hugh Fearnley-Whittingstall as well as members of WWF (the former World Wildlife Fund) have been among those calling for a ban on the practice of discarding.

An international problem

Overfishing is affecting people throughout the world, especially in **developing countries**, meaning countries that are just beginning to develop their economies and industries. Fish—both as a source of income and a staple food—are essential in many developing countries. More than 20 million people in developing countries work in small-scale fisheries. Nearly 70 million more work in the slaughtering and packing industries that process the fish after they are harvested.

More than 90 percent of the catch from developing countries is destined for local markets. In nations along the African coast, for example, up to 70 percent of a person's dietary animal protein comes from fish. Fish provide residents of poor nations with an important source of nutrients and essential fatty acids.

Many of these nations already face a gap between supply and demand, due to increased demand combined with overfishing and dangers to the environment. While fish consumption rose worldwide over the last 30 years, it has actually fallen in Saharan Africa. This is partly due to problems with overfishing, overcrowding of farms, illegal fishing, and lack of management that comes with regional poverty. As populations rise, this gap will only worsen.

As worldwide population has increased, so have the number of fishing boats. At the same time, technology has increased the efficiency of the fishing industry. Sonar, satellite communications, large dragging nets, and miles of strong lines help commercial fishers maximize their catch and income. The increased number of fishing boats and new technology have added to the problem of overfishing, however.

Government regulation

As more and more people fight to catch all the available fish, government regulation and enforcement may be the only way to keep the industry from spiraling out of control. Otherwise, there is a great danger of overfishing. For example, the European Commission Fisheries uses the Common Fisheries Policy (CFP) to regulate fishing among the members of the European Union. The CFP creates **quotas** (limited amounts) for the amounts of each type of fish each member state is allowed to catch, helping to protect fish stocks in the Atlantic Ocean and Mediterranean Sea. The CFP also works to regulate fish grading and packaging and helps to control fish prices.

The policies of the CFP often come under fire from both fishers and conservationists (people concerned about preserving the environment). Fishers complain that the quotas set by the CFP interfere with their ability to make a living. However, it could be argued that if fish stocks are not allowed to recover, more jobs could be lost in the long term. They would like to see control over fishing grounds returned to local governments, rather than a central authority. Conservationists, on the other hand, say that despite CFP quotas, many areas are still overfished. For example, the EU recently cut the amount of endangered cod that can be caught in the Atlantic Ocean by a quarter. Environmentalists were calling for quotas to be halved in order to try to save the fish. They think governments are just avoiding angering the fishing industry. It is difficult to find the right balance.

Starting in 2009, the European Union opened debate among member nations regarding the CFP. In the summer of 2010, it released a report outlining some of the problems, as well as its goals moving forward. According to the report, close to 90 percent of the stocks overseen by the CFP are overfished. Many fish are caught before they are mature enough to reproduce, which adds to the problem. The commission set goals to reduce the size of fishing fleets and to return some control to local authorities. They plan to put new policies in place by 2013.

Case study: Greenpeace

Greenpeace is one of the most visible environmental organizations in the world. The organization was established in the 1970s to promote peace and protest the spread of nuclear weapons. Since then, its efforts have grown to take action on a number of environmental issues, from toxic waste to commercial whaling.

Greenpeace has become known for its role in protecting life in the ocean. Greenpeace vessels, such as its flagship, the *Rainbow Warrior*, seek to disrupt the work of commercial whalers and similar ships. Greenpeace has been criticized for its work. Its tactics are sometimes seen as excessive, and the organization has been accused of distributing false information about the companies it opposes.

Still, Greenpeace provides a valuable service to those interested in environmental issues, such as sustainable seafood (see pages 40 to 45). On its website, Greenpeace maintains its "Red List" of fish sourced from unsustainable fisheries. It provides a wealth of information for both consumers and businesses.

Greenpeace volunteers often face life-threatening situations as they patrol the oceans.

Fish pirates

Yet regulation cannot always solve the problem of overfishing. Unreported and unregulated fishing by companies from China to Europe and Latin America are threatening both large and small fishing operations. These ships fish in areas that are off-limits and they do not report their catches. They "launder" these illegally caught fish by transferring them to legal fishing boats while still at sea. Annual losses to established fisheries are estimated at $15 billion a year, according to a report by the Environmental Justice Foundation.

The situation is particularly serious in Africa. By illegally fishing in restricted waters, pirates are believed to be taking as much as 30 percent of the catch from local fishers in countries such as Somalia and Angola. These countries are particularly hard-hit because they lack the resources to police their waters.

In addition to overfishing these waters, pirates are hunting forbidden varieties. An estimated 700 foreign-owned vessels regularly fish Somalian waters for endangered tuna, shark, and lobster.

The black market

Attempts to protect fish through regulating fishing have brought about a "black market," or illegal selling, of certain species. One such fish is the bluefin tuna. This fish is endangered because of heavy overfishing, and stocks in the Atlantic Ocean and the Mediterranean Sea are severely depleted. Pirate fishers harvest the fish outside of official channels and sell their catch directly to restaurants. In many cases, restaurant owners know the source of the fish is illegal, but they are willing to look the other way to satisfy their customers.

What do you think?
Bluefin tuna

Bluefin tuna is often used in sushi. The Japanese government has successfully blocked efforts by the UN to ban international trade of the fish. Should individual nations have the right to go against international quotas? Should an international organization, such as the UN, have the right to pressure individual nations to comply with their standards?

International organizations that regulate fishing set quotas, or limits, on the amounts of fish allowed. Pirate fishers operate outside that. An effort in 2010 failed to add the bluefin tuna to the international list of endangered species and further limit its catch.

Most restaurants serve caviar that has been produced legally.

Caviar

Caviar is a fast seller on the black market. Caviar is the roe, or eggs, of certain fish. Black caviar, which is highly sought, is produced by sturgeon. The sturgeon is so endangered that catching the fish has been banned by many nations, and limited by others. Despite this, black caviar is available for a high price on the black market in places around the world, especially in Russia. The WWF estimates that about 10 times more sturgeon is caught illegally than is caught in compliance with quotas set to protect it.

Our Toxic Oceans

For years, the health of our oceans has been overlooked. But in recent decades the use of many new technologies, such as satellites, have allowed scientists to study the oceans much more closely, often with alarming results. Solid waste and chemicals have been dumped into the seas by businesses and governments alike. Huge amounts of trash, such as plastic, have found their way into the oceans from individuals and garbage barges. This seagoing trash threatens the life of sea animals—and the people who eat them.

Mercury

One of the most common—and most dangerous—chemicals found in seafood is mercury. Some mercury occurs in rocks and soil, and it gets washed into the water during rains. Mercury is also released into the

How mercury gets to your dinner table

Human-made pollution has increased the amount of mercury in the fish supply to sometimes harmful levels, especially for an unborn child.

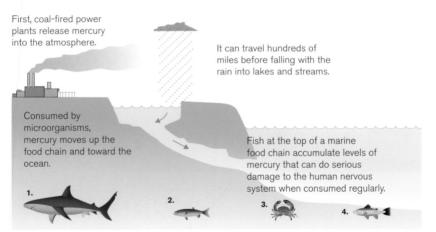

First, coal-fired power plants release mercury into the atmosphere.

It can travel hundreds of miles before falling with the rain into lakes and streams.

Consumed by microorganisms, mercury moves up the food chain and toward the ocean.

Fish at the top of a marine food chain accumulate levels of mercury that can do serious damage to the human nervous system when consumed regularly.

1.   2.   3.   4.

1. LARGE PREDATORY FISH
At the top of the food chain, these fish acquire the highest mercury levels. The FDA recommends that pregnant women avoid swordfish, tilefish, king mackerel, and shark altogether, or risk nervous system damage to an unborn child.

2. SMALLER SALTWATER FISH
These fish such as cod and red snapper can have varying levels of mercury. The FDA recommends pregnant women not consume more than 12 ounces per week.

3. SHELLFISH
These can contain harmful levels of mercury with lobster leading the FDA list.

4. FRESHWATER FISH
Mercury levels vary according to the concentration in the water. Local officials should be contacted to assess mercury risk.

Case study:
Restaurants and mercury

In a recent survey conducted in New York City, seafood dishes from 20 restaurants and sushi bars were tested for mercury content. More than a quarter of the tested items exceeded not only the limits recommended by the U.S. Food and Drug Administration, but they also qualified as hazardous enough to be removed from the market by legal action. A test conducted in Los Angeles showed similar results. At present, tests for mercury have not been conducted in restaurants in other large cities. But since tuna and other fish used in sushi are traded internationally, it is likely that results would be the same.

environment through the burning of fossil fuels—especially coal—in power plants and through the manufacture of chlorine, for which mercury is used in large quantities to extract the chlorine from salt. Fossil fuels are fuels such as coal or oil that have been produced by the slow decay of animals and plants over millions of years. Once mercury has been released into the environment, some of it eventually gets caught up in the water cycle and makes its way into bodies of water such as rivers, lakes, and oceans.

In water, mercury forms a toxin called methylmercury. Over time, tiny organisms (life-forms) absorb this toxin. Small fish species then eat these tainted organisms. Mercury accumulates in their systems, and it may actually kill them. If not, larger carnivorous fish eat them. The carnivores ingest the toxins along with their prey. As a result, the largest fish on top of the food chain have the highest concentration of all pollutants, including mercury. These are the fish we catch and eat.

As we have seen, raw fish preparations, from sushi to ceviche, are popular around the world (see pages 10 and 11). While mercury is dangerous in any fish, it is especially so in those eaten raw. Many governments are confronting this threat.

Other chemicals

A number of heavy metals, such as cadmium, aluminum, and lead, have been released into the sea through industry. In the past, these metals were thought to affect mostly fish in coastal waters. Recently, though, they have been found in sperm whales far from land, from polar regions to the equator. Since sperm whales are at the top of the food chain, many of the fish they eat are already **contaminated**. Contaminated mother whales then pass these chemicals on to their young. This new threat to food chains is still being evaluated.

Solid waste

Each year, the world produces more than 90.7 billion kilograms (200 billion pounds) of plastic. About 10 percent of that ends up in the ocean. Most of this plastic sinks to the ocean floor, where it can harm fish and other sea life. About 30 percent of it floats. Some of this plastic has formed into giant trash islands floating in the Pacific Ocean.

Large circular currents called gyres exist in several places in the oceans. The North Pacific Gyre circulates between North America and Asia. The plastic caught up in this gyre has accumulated into two large masses of trash, called the Great Pacific Garbage Patch. The eastern patch, which floats between California and Hawaii, is twice as large as the state of Texas and 30 meters (100 feet) deep.

A conservationist holds up plastic garbage that has washed up on a beach in Hong Kong.

The western patch, between Hawaii and Japan, is somewhat smaller. These garbage patches are not completely solid. Charles Moore, who discovered the patches, compares them to "plastic soup."

Plastic pollution is having disastrous effects on life in the sea. Bits of plastic break off and are eaten by fish and birds. Schools of fish gather under the plastic, and birds that eat the fish can get caught in the debris. Plastics can release the chemicals they are made up of into the ocean, killing local life. Jellyfish absorb the chemicals and get sick or die. Some of this dead and dying sea life then washes back to shore, endangering those who live on land.

Agricultural runoff

Fertilizers used in farming often end up in the ocean. Farms are overfertilized, and the runoff travels through rivers and groundwater into the sea. There, they affect simple organisms, such as algae, promoting the growth of some while destroying others. The fish that eat these threatened algae can no longer survive, and so the other fish that live on them also die off. More and more areas of the sea are becoming so-called "dead zones," meaning areas where no life can be supported.

What do you think?
Offshore wind farms

A possible new threat to sea creatures is offshore wind farms. Windmills provide a sustainable form of energy, and an alternative to unsustainable energy sources such as fossil fuels. But because large clusters of windmills, called wind farms, can affect people who live nearby, some wind farms have been built in the ocean, away from human habitats. But there they affect the habitats of the native sea life.

Supporters point out that the windmills actually provide new habitats for creatures such as crabs, because their foundations act as artificial reefs. Others worry about how these changes may negatively affect fish presently in these environments. What is the proper balance between the need for "green" energy and the need to conserve these ocean habitats?

Oil

Our modern world runs on petroleum (oil). Fuels refined from petroleum power everything from the family car to jet airplanes. Petroleum products are used to manufacture plastic, asphalt, and house paint. Petroleum is even present in fertilizers and prescription medicines.

As oil becomes harder to find, energy companies search for new oil reserves. Increasingly, that search has taken them deep into our oceans. These offshore wells are difficult to build and maintain. The drilling platform is often thousands of feet above the ocean floor. Even well-maintained rigs regularly leak crude oil into the surrounding water.

Accidents

Transporting oil can be risky as well. Oil tankers transport millions of gallons of oil. Accidents can be disastrous. One of the largest oil spills occurred in 1989 when the *Exxon Valdez* oil tanker struck an offshore reef and spilled an estimated 95 to 120 million liters (25 to 32 million gallons) of oil into Prince William Sound, off the coast of Alaska.

The spill killed thousands of sea creatures. Experts estimate the dead wildlife at 250,000 seabirds, 2,800 sea otters, 300 seals, and 22 whales. While fish can often survive such disasters, their eggs cannot, and billions of salmon and herring eggs were destroyed. The results of the spill were long lasting. Twenty years after the spill, scientists found the area had still not returned to its former condition.

Another spill occurred in February 1996 when the *Sea Empress* was grounded off the southwest coast of Wales in the UK. About 72,000 tons of oil was spilled. This affected wildlife and people in the fishing industry. Sea birds were badly affected in the first few weeks after the spill and thousands died. Fishing was banned by the government immediately after the spill. A program of sampling was carried out to determine how many commercially fished species had been contaminated by oil. The ban was soon lifted once it was discovered that shellfish numbers were not too badly affected. The ban remained for longer for other species, however.

Case study:
Deepwater Horizon

On April 20, 2010, the oil rig *Deepwater Horizon*, 64 kilometers (40 miles) off the coast of Louisiana, suffered an explosion and fire that killed 11 workers and injured 17 more. Within 36 hours, the rig collapsed and sank about 1,500 meters (5,000 feet) below, to the sea floor.

The accident created a massive oil spill, now considered the largest in the history of the petroleum industry. The exposed pipe poured more than 50,000 barrels of oil a day into the Gulf of Mexico. Efforts to cap the pipe did not succeed until nearly three months after the explosion. By that time, nearly 5 million barrels of oil had escaped into the Gulf.

At the time of this writing, the effects of the spill on sea life and the local **ecology** and economy were still being estimated. The animals most at risk were local seabirds and turtles. By October 2010, the U.S. government had documented nearly 600 dead turtles and had rescued and released 537 more. Nearly 100 dolphins and whales had been killed. The Gulf of Mexico is a major source of wild shrimp, and seafood producers in the area are just beginning to feel the impact on their livelihood. Oil seeped from the Gulf into freshwaters in Louisiana and the nearby state of Mississippi.

In August of 2010, researchers found that a new strain of microbe (microscopic life-form) had developed in the Gulf region. This microbe was actually eating the dispersed oil, breaking it down. While such microbes can deplete the oxygen of ocean waters, this seemed not to be the case. It was a sign that recovery might happen more quickly than expected. Still, as with the *Exxon Valdez* spill, it is likely that the effects of this spill will be felt for many years to come.

The oil spill from the *Deepwater Horizon* drilling station will affect marine life in the area for years to come.

A Sustainable Future

Conservation is not a new practice. Conservation of natural resources, including land, water, and the creatures that live there, has its roots in the 19th century. By the 1970s, many people developed an interest in issues regarding the environment and ecology. During this time, the first measures that led to the Common Fisheries Policy, which set standards for fishing conservation throughout Europe (see page 30), were in the process of being developed.

In recent years, an emphasis on conservation and sustainable practices has taken root in a number of types of food production. Producing food sustainably means producing it in such a way that there is minimal harm to the environment—while still feeding as many people as possible. Fishing is no exception.

You need to be an educated consumer to make the right choices at a supermarket. Don't hesitate to ask lots of questions when buying food such as fresh fish. You can even come prepared with a list of questions to ask about certain types of fish.

Both wild fisheries and aquaculture are working to find ways to catch and raise fish in ways that will ensure their availability for many years to come.

Aquaculture is a sustainable practice, because young fish are being raised all the time. As you have read, though, unless practiced responsibly, aquaculture can have negative effects on the environment (see pages 22 and 23). Fishing can also be sustainable, as long as fishers maintain quotas and do not overfish depleted stocks.

Ethical choices for consumers

Unfortunately, sustainable practices do not come without a price. Consumers have grown used to having a wide choice of seafood available in markets year round. But, like other foods, many fish are seasonal. They have a natural life cycle and are available at different times. Wild salmon, for example, are often caught when they are returning to their native spawning grounds to mate. While this sounds cruel, as long the fishing is done responsibly, it does not affect overall fish stocks. But when fishers go against these natural cycles, this can lead to overfishing. To prevent this problem, consumers have to accept that they may not be able to get every kind of fish year round.

In addition, sustainable practices are usually more expensive than the more efficient "factory" fishing. This makes it tempting for consumers to buy cheaper, "factory" types of fish. Consumers may have to find a balance between making ethical choices and finding good prices.

Case study: New protections in the United Kingdom

In 2009 the UK government took greater control of its coastal waters with the Marine and Coastal Access Act. The act protects marine habitats throughout the United Kingdom. It also created the Marine Management Organization to manage and protect coastal and marine waters. This organization includes systems to reform both ocean and freshwater fisheries.

In order to make sure rules and laws are being followed, the Marine Management Organization coordinates a program for monitoring and enforcement of fishing activities. This includes the inspection of fishing vessels, both at sea and in port. It also includes the inspection of fishing industry premises, fish markets, and other related locations. There is also a program of aerial surveillance, as well as a satellite monitoring system that tracks the positions of fishing vessels over 15 meters (49 feet) in length.

Responsible retailing

The efforts of fisheries to become more sustainable need to be met by those who sell fish, both to the public and to restaurants. Restaurant owners need to be aware of which fish are endangered and only offer sustainable selections.

Environment watch

Seafood Watch

Seafood Watch is a program of the Monterey Bay Aquarium in northern California. Its website serves as a resource for consumers, retailers, and restaurants to learn more about issues that affect fishing and the environment. The site offers suggestions of what seafood is safe to buy, what you should avoid, and what substitutions you can make. For example, in place of Chilean sea bass (see page 27), Seafood Watch suggests farmed cobia (see page 19) or wild sablefish or black cod from Alaska or British Columbia. Among its other resources is a monthly sustainable seafood recipe from famous chefs such as Rick Bayless and Alton Brown.

Organizations such as the Monterey Bay Aquarium have gotten involved with an effort to educate consumers about safe, sustainable seafood.

Companies such as EcoFish out of Dover, New Hampshire, have made efforts to fish and distribute seafood in an environmentally responsible way. EcoFish sells seafood to restaurants and retailers, and helps to support sustainable fisheries, both wild and aquaculture, and help reverse the decline of marine biodiversity by encouraging a shift in consumer demand away from over-exploited fisheries.

EcoFish also supports marine conservation efforts through collaboration with conservation, research, and educational organizations worldwide. The company was launched in 1999 to provide more environmentally responsible seafood in response to overfishing and a need for better management of ocean resources.

Case study:
Wild Planet Foods

Wild Planet Foods is one of the growing number of seafood marketers to respond to consumers' desire for responsibly sourced fish. Wild Planet produces canned seafood, such as tuna, salmon, and sardines. All of its fish are caught wild. On its website, the company even lists the methods used to catch each variety of fish it sells!

Wild Planet's story parallels the rising interest in sustainability in the population as a whole. In 2003 William Carvalho and Bill McCarthy decided they needed to follow more sustainable practices in their seafood business. They cut their ties to fisheries that used methods that damaged marine habitats or resulted in wasteful bycatch. That included fishers who use harmful trawling methods. In 2005 they founded Wild Planet.

Needless to say, Wild Planet promotes the sustainability of its product. It offers links to the Monterey Bay Aquarium Seafood Watch program and proudly announces that many of its products are on Seafood Watch's "Super Green" list of sustainable seafood options. Its shrimp and salmon products have been certified as sustainable by the Marine Stewardship Council, an organization that certifies fisheries worldwide.

Wild Planet recognizes that being sustainable is not enough. So, it also claims that its product is higher in omega-3 fats, lower in mercury, and tastes better than other brands. It offers a series of charts and customer testimonials to support its claims. Of course, much of this is simply advertising. But since Wild Planet oversees production from the fishing boat to final canning, there may be merit to its claims.

Catch shares

In the 1970s, starting in Australia, New Zealand, and Iceland, a new approach to managing fisheries began to take hold.

Known as "catch shares," or Limited Access Privilege Programs, this type of system dedicates a secure share of fish to an individual fisher, community, or fishery association. Each year before the season begins, fishers know how much fish they are allowed to take as part of the fishery's Total Allowable Catch.

Fishers are often allowed to buy and sell shares in order to maximize their profit. This helps drive the fishery to an efficient level. It also rewards innovative fishers who can lower costs and deliver a quality product that will fetch a good price on the market.

On November 4, 2010, the National Oceanic and Atmospheric Administration of the United States released its own national policy encouraging the consideration and use of catch shares as a fishery management tool that can help rebuild fisheries. Jane Lubchenco of the NOAA said, "Catch share programs have proven to be powerful tools to transform fisheries, making them prosperous, stable and sustainable parts of our nation's strategy for healthy and resilient ocean ecosystems."

FAO and MSC

The Food and Agriculture Organization of the United Nations (FAO) issues guidelines for the eco-friendly labeling of foods. The only major international program for eco-friendly fisheries is the Marine Stewardship Council (MSC). The MSC was established in 1996. It uses independent firms to test fisheries against its principles and criteria. The principles and criteria are: the fishery must have a healthy and productive stock, the ecosystem function must be healthy, and there must be effective management of the fishery. The distinctive half-checkmark, half-fish, blue-and-white label means the seafood product is certified as sustainable seafood by the Marine Stewardship Council.

Artisan fishing

"Artisan fishing" is a term used to describe small-scale commercial or subsistence fishing, meaning fishing that is done to feed oneself and one's family. The term particularly applies to groups that use traditional techniques such as rod and tackle, arrows and harpoons, throw nets, and drag nets and small traditional fishing boats. Artisan fishing is not sport fishing, though it may use similar practices.

Artisan fishing is viewed as a good alternative to large-scale commercial fisheries because it is less intensive and less stressful on fish populations. Some people argue that artisan fishing produces a healthier product, since there is a closer connection between the fisher and the fish. Others hold the opposite view: they believe that artisan fishing is less safe because these fisheries sometimes suffer from inadequate refrigeration and processing facilities. Since the goal of artisan fishing is more local consumption, though, this is rarely a problem.

Artisan fishing is a sustainable practice that is practiced in many cultures. Most of the fish caught is consumed locally.

How Can I Make a Difference?

It is easy to feel overwhelmed by the size of the growing seafood crisis. But there are many small steps individuals can make that will help lead toward larger changes.

Consumer choice

From what you have read, you may think the oceans will soon be fished out. But this does not have to be the case. Many species of fish are doing well, and more and more fisheries and retailers are acting responsibly. If this issue is important to you, you can support their work every time you shop or dine out. As a consumer, you have a lot of control over what stores sell and what restaurants serve. These businesses exist to serve the customer, and what the customer does not choose to buy, they will not sell. You can use the power of your wallet to encourage businesses to buy responsibly.

Be an informed consumer. With a little effort, you can stay aware of which fish are safe to consume and which are endangered. Resources such as Seafood Watch (see pages 42 and 43) offer regular updates on the state of fish stocks. Refer to the listings for this site and others at the end of this book (see pages 54 and 55).

Feel free to ask questions at the market. Ask where your fish comes from and whether it is wild or farmed. If your local grocer does not have the answers, you can find one that does. When you are dining out, ask questions about menu items. Restaurants respond quickly to diners' choices. If no one orders the Chilean sea bass, it will come off the menu.

Eat lower on the food chain

Salmon and tuna are appetizing choices. But these large fish consume more food per pound of growth than smaller fish, such as trout or tilapia. Because of their diet of smaller fish, wild salmon and tuna carry a greater chance of mercury contamination as well.

Smaller fish can be prepared in many different ways, providing greater variety for daily eating. Reserve larger fish for "special occasion" eating, and introduce more of the smaller fish into your diet. Many of the smallest fish, such as sardines, are also the healthiest choices available.

Recognize the cost

Less expensive choices may turn out to be more costly in the long run. Seafood that is responsibly raised or caught may be more expensive per pound that other fish, but these methods are better for the fish, workers, and the environment. Don't always put price first. You can develop habits now that will lead you to continue to make responsible choices throughout your adult life.

By eating fish lower on the food chain, diners can help to reduce their impact on fishing resources.

Hold governments accountable

Like stores and restaurants, governments respond to people's demands. They may be slow to move, but input by citizens is one thing that may force them into action. Many of the upcoming reforms of the Common Fisheries Policy (see page 30) were prompted by the concerns of ordinary citizens.

The value of government regulation is hotly debated. Many people are against any regulation at all. They believe such regulations slow the growth of business, and they point out that many countries and fishers operate outside such restrictions (see pages 32 and 33). Though this may be true, only governments have the power to set guidelines and regulations for the fishing industry. They can ensure that the food that reaches our markets is safe and properly inspected. Governments have access to controls that the ordinary citizen does not.

Get involved

Many organizations are working to protect our oceans and develop solutions that meet the needs of developing countries. Some of these organizations are listed in the resources at the end of this book (see pages 54 and 55). Take time to learn about them and the work they do. Then make up your own mind about the issues that are important to you.

More and more small-scale fisheries are developing throughout the world. Their methods of fishing and farming are often better for the environment and the health of their workers. Not only that, but their fish are also generally tastier than those sold by large producers.

Though you may not make the shopping or dining decisions in your family, you can influence the decisions made by your parents. Marketers often target kids and teens because of the power they exert over their parents' purchasing. If these issues are important to you, make your wishes known!

Small steps can make a big difference

In this book, we have looked at some of the ethical considerations involved in catching and raising fish and other seafood. There are no easy answers. "Small" does not always mean good, any more than "big" always means bad. As consumers show their interest in these issues, more and more large producers are changing their methods of catching, raising, and handling our food. The Chinese philosopher Lao-tzu famously said, "A journey of a thousand miles begins with a single step." Every individual can exercise his or her choice through small steps, as well as supporting the bigger steps that will lead to bigger changes.

There are many ways for people to make their voices heard and influence their food supply. But anyone can start by first becoming educated on where food comes from.

Be Informed!

Use the information on these pages as a beginner's practical guide for buying seafood. Also use these pages and Internet resources to get to know some of the terms that you may encounter at grocery stores and fish markets. Remember to always ask questions when you buy. If the store doesn't have any safe, sustainable options, talk to the worker behind the counter or even the manager. After all, you are a customer and the things customers say have a strong effect on the kinds of foods store managers choose to stock!

Advice for buying healthy seafood ethically

- Avoid seafood from far away—more fossil fuels have been used to ship it. It also means the seafood was likely frozen and thawed more than once, which will affect the taste.

- Avoid predator fish that live long lives, such as sharks, swordfish, Chilean sea bass, and tuna. Since they are older and larger, they usually have the highest levels of mercury.

- Eat farmed seafood that is fed vegetable—not animal—protein. Good species include tilapia, catfish, and carp.

- Quality and environmental standards in North America and Europe tend to be higher, so seafood farmed in those regions tends to be a more reliable choice.

- Organically farmed salmon, trout, and cod are usually not as densely farmed, nor treated with as many chemicals.

- Choosing seafood at the lower end of the food chain is the best choice (mackerel, oysters, etc.), as it is better for your health and the health of the world's oceans.

Good seafood fishing methods

Knowing how your seafood was caught is a major step toward choosing seafood in an ethical manner. Some methods have much less impact on the environment than others.

Hook and line

This method is simply a baited hook at the end of a line. Fish caught using this method are also sometimes called pole-caught or hand-line-caught. With this method unwanted fish can usually be returned to the water without harm.

Trolling

Trolling is when a boat trails several lines (multiple hook-and-line arrangement) at a time to catch fish in certain areas. As with hook-and-line fishing, the fisher can throw back unwanted species without harming them. Trolling is often used to catch Pacific salmon, albacore tuna, and mahi-mahi. This is different from "trawling," which involves towing a net. Using nets brings in unwanted species and causes a greater amount of harm to the environment.

Bad seafood fishing methods

The following fishing methods are considered the most unethical due to their tendency to kill species that are not targeted and due to their high impact on the environment.

Drift nets

Drift nets and ghost nets are hug nets that entangle unwanted species, including even seabirds. They were banned by the United Nations in 1992, but small drift nets are still allowed in coastal waters in the United States and Europe.

Dynamite and poison

Dynamite and cyanide poison are sometimes used to stun reef fish and make them easier to catch alive. This can kill precious coral reefs. Many tropical fish are captured this way.

Bottom-trawls

Bottom-trawling is also known as dragging. In this method a net is towed across the seafloor. Many unwanted species are caught, and the seafloor is disturbed and even destroyed.

Good seafood to eat

The following is a list of seafood to choose if you are worried about eating ethically and having a smaller impact on the environment.

Arctic char	Mullet	Squid
Barramundi	Oysters	Trout
Pacific halibut	Mussels	Blue whiting
Herring	Pollock	Capelin
Jellyfish	Sablefish	Anchoveta
Mackerel	Sardines	Sand lance

Glossary

antibiotic drug used to kill bacteria and treat infections

aquaculture underwater agriculture; raising of aquatic plants and animals in natural or controlled water environments

bycatch unwanted marine creatures that are caught in the nets while fishing for another species

carnivorous creature that eats flesh; meat eater

commercial related to business and the buying and selling of goods

conservation protection of natural things such as animals and plants to prevent them from being destroyed

consumer someone who buys and uses products and services

contaminated something contaminated has had a harmful substance added to it

deplete reduce the amount of something that is present

developing country poor country whose citizens are mostly farmers and that wants to become more economically and socially advanced

ecology way in which plants, animals, and people are related to each other and their environment; also the scientific study of this

ecosystem all the animals and plants in a particular area and the way in which they relate to each other and their environment

endangered species species at risk of extinction, and often designated as such by an official organization

ethical relating to principles of what is right and wrong

fertilizer substance that is put on the soil to make plants grow

fishery part of the sea where fish are caught in large numbers

flash freeze process of freezing food rapidly, which allows it to be stored a very long time at freezing temperatures

fleet group of ships

food chain all animals and plants in a group where one is eaten by another, which in turn is eaten by another, and so on

habitat natural home of a plant or animal

mercury heavy, silver-white, poisonous metal that is liquid at room temperature and is a chemical element with the symbol Hg

mollusk type of sea or land animal that has a soft body covered by a hard shell, such as a snail, mussel, or octopus

Neanderthal early, prehistoric type of human being that is now extinct

omega-3 fatty acids type of polyunsaturated fatty acid that is found primarily in fish, fish oils, vegetable oils, and leafy green vegetables, and that seems to reduce the risk of stroke and heart attack

overfishing act of taking too many fish from an area of water, so that the number of fish in the area becomes too low

paleontologist scientist who studies fossils of plants and animals

parasite plant or animal that lives on or in another plant or animal and gets food from it

pollution substances that make air, water, and soil dangerously dirty

process act of making food, materials, or goods ready to be sold or used by preserving or changing them in some way

protein natural substance that exists in food such as meat, eggs, fish, and beans, and that your body needs in order to grow and stay strong and healthy

quota official limit on the number or amount of something that is allowed in a particular period of time

regulate control an activity or process, usually by rules

sonar equipment on a ship or submarine that uses sound waves to find out the position of underwater objects

species group of animals or plants whose members are similar and can breed to produce young

staple forming the greatest or most important part of something; the basic food a diet is built on is a staple food for that diet

stock total amount of something that is available to be used in a particular area

sustainable able to continue without causing damage to the environment

toxin poisonous substance, especially one produced by bacteria that causes disease

trawling fishing by pulling a special, wide net behind a boat

Further Information

Books

Baur, Gene. *Farm Sanctuary: Changing Hearts and Minds About Animals and Food*. New York, NY: Touchstone, 2008.

Clover, Charles. *The End of the Line: How Overfishing Is Changing the World and What We Eat*. Berkeley, CA: University of California Press, 2008.

Greenberg, Paul. *Four Fish: The Future of the Last Wild Food*. New York, NY: Penguin Press, 2010.

Grescoe, Taras. *Bottomfeeder: How to Eat Ethically in a World of Vanishing Seafood*. New York, NY: Bloomsbury USA, 2008.

Issenberg, Sasha. *The Sushi Economy: Globalization and the Making of a Modern Delicacy*. New York, NY: Gotham, 2008.

K., Laura. *Food* (*Opposing Viewpoints* series). Farmington Hills, MI: Greenhaven Press, 2006.

Pauly, Daniel. *5 Easy Pieces: The Impact of Fisheries on Marine Ecosystems*. Washington, DC: Island Press, 2010.

Pollan, Michael. *Food Rules: An Eater's Manual*. New York, NY: Penguin (Non-Classics), 2009.

Schlosser, Eric, and Charles Wilson. *Chew On This: Everything You Don't Want to Know About Fast Food*. Boston, MA: Houghton Mifflin, 2007.

Sherrow, Victoria, and Alan Marzilli. *Food Safety* (*Point/Counterpoint* series). New York, NY: Chelsea House, 2008.

Weber, Karl, and Participant Media, eds. *Food, Inc.: A Participant Guide*. Cambridge, MA: PublicAffairs Books, 2009.

DVDs

The Cove. Santa Monica, CA: Lions Gate Entertainment, 2009.

The End of the Line. New York, NY: Docurama, 2009.

Websites

www.fishbase.org
You can find information on thousands of seafood species on this website.

www.fishonline.org
Created by the Marine Conservation Society, this website contains guides to buying and eating fish, as well information about fishing and farming methods.

www.msc.org
The Marine Stewardship Council is an organization that works to encourage and certify seafood from sustainable sources. The website contains news and information about the MSC and seafood industry

www.seachoice.org
SeaChoice has information on Canadian fisheries and seafood.

www.montereybayaquarium.org/cr/seafoodwatch.aspx
Monterey Bay Aquarium's Seafood Watch website is a great way to brush up on seafood-related issues.

www.wildplanetfoods.com
Wild Planet foods is committed to providing sustainably caught, wild seafood while supporting the conservation of wild marine ecosystems.

Topics for further research

Reliable sources
Conduct further research to find reliable sources of information on what kinds of seafood are good food choices from a health and environmental point of view. Use the websites listed above to begin your research.

What's real?
What causes the colors of various kinds of seafood? Do farmed seafood products and their wild counterparts eat the same foods? Does their flesh look the same? Explore these questions for yourself.

Seafood diet
Find and try some recipes for sustainable seafood. Try to incorporate seafood into your diet twice a week in place of other meats and see if it makes a difference in how you feel after a couple of weeks.

Local sources
Find out the sources your local stores and restaurants use to supply their seafood. Research the seafood suppliers and whether they are considered sources of sustainable seafood.

The *Deepwater Horizon* oil spill
Do further research on 2010's massive *Deepwater Horizon* oil spill in the Gulf of Mexico. What is the current assessment of the environmental impact of the disaster? How has it continued to affect the seafood and seafood industry in the area? How have nearby people been affected?

Index